Gary & Cynthia both know what hard work is all about, from their days of working at

UPS and the Post Office. This is the attitude they brought to their new venture; the building of —Schmidt Rental Property‖. In 1994 they bought their first 2 homes. By the end of that first year they had 18 units. In 1995 they added 20 more. They learned the secrets of finding and buying property under value. They shopped the market for foreclosures and for motivated sellers. They discovered one very important point; you have to make your money when you buy investment property.

By this time, Cynthia had left the Post Office and was a full time landlord. She had definitely caught the fever; the real estate fever! They maintained and expanded the business, one house at a time, one building at a time. They have accumulated 75 units and are collecting over $500,000.00 a year in rent. By the year 2000, Gary retired from the UPS. Now they both shared in their dream of self-employment.

 Their 75 units consisted of mostly single family homes, but they have also owned apartment houses and duplexes.

TESTIMONIAL

This course teaches you the basic ingredient of being a landlord; how to collect your rent. There are dozens of real estate investment courses out there that tell you how to buy real estate, but that is only one small part of the larger equation. Some of the information provided could be a formula for foreclosure and failure, if you do not know how to collect all your rent.

Collecting rent can be an arcane and complex procedure that this course puts into an easy to understand, step by step process. It put me on a continuing road to real estate investment success. The Schmidt's course really works! I would say that any landlord that is serious about trying to retrieve lost rent should buy this course.

Wayne C.

Naperville, IL

Full-Time Landlord

MISTAKES AT THE COURT HEARING

1] Not picking up proof of services before court date. The first thing the judge will ask is, —Do you have proof of service? If you do not, your whole day starts out wrong. There is tons of stress the day of court so you want to be 100% prepared.

2) Adding utilities and damages to the amount being sought. Remember that this court concerns, court costs and possession and rent due only. If we include amounts for anything else, the judge can dismiss the case, thus costing you more time and money.

3) Talking to tenant(s) in the hallway prior to the judge's decision. The talking is over when we have to file for eviction. We let the judge do the job now. We've gone this far and are confident the decision will be in our favor.

4) Surrendering a money judgment just to get their place back - most untrained landlords tend to think this way. After all, they don't know how to get the money judgment satisfied anyway. That is why the landlord profession gets a bad reputation from non-trained landlords in the courts.

5) Not having the order ready to fill in the judge's decision at the podium. Being prepared is everything here. You do not want to be fumbling through paperwork in front of the judge. Our manuals will train you to have your orders all filled out, except the space where you fill in what the judge orders on that day.

6) Sending a person not listed as a plaintiff(s) to represent the plaintiff that is not an attorney. If there are two plaintiffs, only one has to appear in court. However, we can never have a relative or friend represent us.

7) Not scheduling the sheriff after the decision is made in the Forcible Detainer for removal. This may cost you more time if the tenant does not vacate when ordered.

8) Not having a daily amount of rent computed in case the judge gives them longer. You can add the daily amount to the original amount being sought. Our manuals will train you to have the total amount of rent due, already computed to the amount of time the judge may stay the possession order.

9) Addressing the tenant at the podium— which is a NO-NO.

TABLE OF CONTENTS

DISCLAIMER

This publication is intended to provide and authoritative information with regard to the subject matter covered. It is offered with the understanding rendering <u>legal,</u> <u>accounting,</u> or other professional services. *If legal advice or other expert assistance is required, the services of a competent professional should be retained*. From the Declaration of Principle jointly adopted of the American Bar Association and a committee of Publishers and Associations. Every effort has been made to reflect current tax law and interpretations as of the date of publication of this book. However, this is a dynamic field of endeavor in which new laws are enacted, tax laws are constantly changing and old laws precede laws, Revenue Rulings, and Treasury Policy

Collect Back Rent Eviction Process is for instructional use only.

Copyright 2020 Cynthia Schmidt

PLAYERS

Attorney -An attorney is someone who can help with your legal problems by acting as your advocate and can represent you in court and in negotiation settlements.

Bailiff— Court appointed security guard; he/she maintains silence in the courts and monitors court cases. Also, assists judge with their needs

Circuit Clerk— Circuit Clerk is responsible for creating, managing and updating court files. When you want to put something in a court file, see a court file, obtain court dates, the Circuit Clerk's office is where you would go.

Constable-An officer of the peace in a town or township.

Judge— The judge is the person who presides over the courtroom. In most cases, the judge makes all final decisions and approves all agreements. When a judge makes a decision or a finding, it has the force of law. The judge sets and enforces court rules and in some courthouses, the judge decides when cases are scheduled.

Justice of the Peace— Local public officer having authority to try civil and criminal cases.

Magistrate-Civil officer charged with the administration of the law.

Process Server—A person and/or agency that is bonded, and has legal authority to serve documents.

Pro-se— A person who is not represented by an attorney and is involved by being either the plaintiff or defendant.

Sheriff-The sheriff's main duty is to keep the peace and enforce the law. The sheriff can serve court documents and also enforces judge's orders.

TERMS

Accrued Rent-Rent that has accumulated since the serving of the quit or pay notice to day of possession.

Adjournment—Postponement.

Bench Warrant— Order issued by the judge for arrest and bond on an individual.

Body Attachment-An order of arrest issued when a party fails to appear to a Rule to Show Cause hearing.

Commingle-To mix or mingle together.

Contempt-When a person fails to follow a court order which directs him/her to do or not to do something; he/she can be held in contempt of court.

Continuance— Postponement of a hearing or trial to a later date.

Cover Sheet— Top sheet in court files.

Creditor— Person (s) that are owed money.

Damages— A sum awarded by the court as compensation for an injury.

Debtor— Person who owes the money.

Default— Person(s) were served court documents but failed to appear.

Default Judgment— Defendant(s) fail to appear, judgment is rendered.

Defendant— Person being sued.

Dismissal- The removal of a claim from the court prior to a trial.

Ejectment—Removal from property.

Evicted— Defendant(s) ordered by the judge to move out of residence in question.

Eviction— Court proceedings to remove the tenants and be awarded money damages.

Forcible Detainer— Lawsuit between the landlord and tenant concerning rent and possession.

Immediate Possession— A procedure for expedited return of real or personal property.

Judgment— Money that has been awarded by the judge.

Jurisdiction- Whether the court in a particular state has power to hear a case or to order someone to do something depends upon whether it has —jurisdiction‖.

Motion- A written request to the judge after a lawsuit has been started.

Non–Service— Process server or sheriff was unable to serve court documents.

Open Account-A running billing for goods or services rendered under a pre-existing agreement between parties.

Party-Any person suing or being sued.

Possession-When the plaintiff(s) regain the property back.

Post-Judgment Proceedings—Proceedings after the judgment has been awarded to retrieve the judgment and court costs.

Pro-Se—Person who represents themselves in court, without an attorney.

Process Server—Sheriff or licensed server that serves court documents.

Service-Serving the court documents.

Small Claims—Lawsuit concerning rent, damages and unpaid utilities.

Statute-The law that the state legislature or federal government enacted on a particular subject.

Third-Party Respondent—Financial institution with which the judgment debtor has an account.

Trial—Defendant(s) have a chance to plead their position in the lawsuit.

We talk with landlords from all across the country. One concern that we hear over and over is that the departing tenant or even a previous tenant cannot be located. Landlords can't take advantage of all the knowledge and information in our training course if they don't have a current address.

We agree that this is an integral part of the process. It is the first step towards getting back the income you already earned but haven't realized. So, here are some tips that can help.

1) The first thing we do when a tenant moves out of our unit is to notify the Post Office that the unit is vacant and we are the owner, and do not want any mail delivered to this address. In the past we've had our previous tenants coming back to our property daily to get the mail. We don't want these people to come back, especially if we had to evict them.

We are entitled to this information if we are representing ourselves in litigation or prospective litigation and the address is needed for the service of legal process. This is huge. Take advantage of it.

2) We have good luck finding former tenants when we search the court records.

50 State Overview

For the first time ever, the Collect Back Rent Landlord Training Course has added a concise, easy to understand summary of the eviction and debt collection process for all 50 states. We are very excited about this opportunity.

As we studied the 50 states, we noticed that there are many more similarities than differences when it comes the eviction process and the collecting of our back rent. This gave us confidence that our program can work for everyone.

Simply study your state's overview page and then apply the principles to our training course. There is a basic, common thread that weaves through all the states.

Tenants have to pay the rent and take care of the residence in all other matters. If they fail to do so, we have to give them notice and a time frame to correct any infractions. If that is not done, then we are entitled to regain possession and seek monetary relief in the courts. The forms as well are very similar.

Alabama

Non-Payment - 7 days if lease fails to state a time.

Infractions of the Lease - 14 days

End of Tenancy - Less than one year - 10 days. Over one year - 30 days.

Evictions-Unlawful Detainer

1) Complaint

2) Summons

3) Writ of Restitution (Possession)

Alaska

Notices   Non-Payment - 7 days.

Infractions of the Lease - 10 days.

End of Tenancy - 30 days.

Eviction-Forcible Entry and Detainer

1) Summons

2) Complaint

3) Answer

4) Landlord-tenant handbook

Arizona

Non-Payment - 5 days.

Infractions of the Lease - 10 days.

End of Tenancy - 30 days.

Eviction-Forcible Detainer

1) Complaint

2) Summons

3) Writ of Restitution (Possession)

Arkansas

Non-Payment - 3 days (civil) - 10 days (criminal)

Infractions of the Lease - 3 days

End of Tenancy - 30 days.

Evictions-Unlawful Detainer (civil)

1) Complaint

2) Summons

3) Writ of Possession

Eviction - Failure to Vacate (criminal)

California

Non-Payment - 3 days.

Infractions of the Lease - 3 days

End of Tenancy - 30 days month to month. 60 days if tenant has resided over 1 year. 90 days rent subsidized.

Evictions-Unlawful Detainer

1) Complaint

2) Summons

3) Pre-judgment Claim of Right to Possession.

4) Writ of Restitution.

Colorado

Non-Payment - 3 days.

Infractions of the Lease - 10 days

End of Tenancy - 1 year or longer - 90 days 6 months to 1 year - 30 days

Evictions-Forcible Entry and Detainer

1) Complaint

2) Summons

3) Writ of Restitution. (Possession)

Connecticut

Non-Payment - 3 days.

Infractions of the Lease - 10 days

End of Tenancy - Month to month - 30 days Year lease - 60 days

Evictions-Unlawful Detainer

1) Complaint

2) Summons

3) Appearance (answer)

4) Order to vacate (execution)

Delaware

Non-Payment - 5 days.

Infractions of the Lease - 7 days

End of Tenancy - 60 days

Evictions-Forcible Entry and Detainer

1) Summons

2) Complaint

3) Notice of Hearing

4) Writ of Restitution (Possession)

District of Columbia

Non-Payment - 30 days

Infractions of the Lease - 30 days

End of Tenancy - 30 days

 Evictions - Forcible Detainer

 1) Complaint

 2) Summons

3) Writ of Restitution (possession

Florida

Non-Payment - 3 business days.

Infractions of the Lease - 7 days

End of Tenancy - One year - 60 days month to month 15 days

Evictions-Court 1 (Possession)

Court 2 (Possession and rent due) Court 1

1) Complaint for Removal

2) 5 - Day Summons

3) Final Judgment for Removal

4) Writ of Possession

Georgia

Non-Payment - Landlord may proceed to Dispossessory

Infractions of the Lease -Cure or Quit Notice.

End of Tenancy - Month to month 30 days One year 60 days.

Evictions-Dispossessory Proceedings.

1) Dispossessory Affidavit.

2) Summons

3) Writ of Possession

Hawaii

Non-Payment - 5 days

Infractions of the Lease - 10 days

End of Tenancy - Month to month - 45 days. One year lease - 28 days.

Evictions-Unlawful Detainer

1) Complaint

2) Unlawful Detainer Summons

3) Writ of Possession

Idaho

Non-Payment - 3 days

Infractions of the Lease - Fixed-term lease - 3 days

End of Tenancy - 30 days

Evictions - Forcible Entry and Unlawful Detainer

1) Complaint

2) Summons

3) Writ of Restitution

Illinois

Non-Payment - 5 days

Infractions of the Lease - 10 days

End of Tenancy - 30 days

Evictions - Forcible Detainer and Entry

1) Cover Sheet

2) Complaint

3) Summons

4) Affidavit of Non-Military Service

5) Order of Possession

Indiana

Non-Payment - 10 days

Infractions of the Lease - Reasonable time to cure

End of Tenancy - 30 days

Evictions

1) Notice of Claim

2) Affidavit for Immediate Possession

3) Affidavit of Non-Military

4) Order for Possession

Iowa

Non-Payment - 3 days

Infractions of the Lease - 7 days

End of Tenancy - Month to month or longer - 30 days

Evictions - Forcible Entry and Detainer

1) Complaint

2) Summons

3) Writ of Possession

Kansas

Non-Payment - 3 days

Infractions of the Lease - 14 days

End of Tenancy - Month to month or longer - 30 days but only 15 days if tenant is in military.

Evictions - Forcible Detainer

1) Petition (Eviction)

2) Petition (Eviction and Rent)

3) Evictions Summons

4) Writ of Restitution

Louisiana

Non-Payment - 5 days.

Infractions of the Lease - 5 days.

End of Tenancy - Month to month 10 days before end of term.

Evictions - Rule for Possession

1) Complaint

2) Summons

3) Judgment of Possession

Maine

Non-Payment - 7 days, must be 7 days in arrears.

Infractions of the Lease - 7 days.

End of Tenancy - 30 days.

Evictions - Forcible Detainer

1) Complaint

2) Summons

3) Writ of Possession

Maryland

Non-Payment - Landlord may proceed directly to District Court for Order of Repossession.

Infractions of the Lease - 30 days non-curable

End of Tenancy - 30 days

Evictions - Forcible Entry and Detainer

1) Complaint

2) Summons

3) Affidavit of Military Service

4) Warrant of Possession

Massachusetts

Non-Payment - 10 day Tenant has 10 days after receiving notice. Tenancy terminates on the 14th day.

Infractions of the Lease - 30 days.

End of Tenancy - Month to month - 30 days year lease 60 days.

Evictions - Summary Process

1) Complaint

2) Summons

3) Answer (tenant has 7 days)

4) Writ of Restitution

Michigan

Non-Payment - 7 days.

Infractions of the Lease - Damage to property creating a health hazard 7days Lease Infraction - 30 days.

End of Tenancy - 30 days.

Evictions - Complaint for Eviction

1) Complaint

2) Summons

3) Writ of Restitution after 10 days.

Minnesota

Non-Payment - 14 days.

Infractions of the Lease - 14 days.

End of Tenancy - Notice must be at least as long as the rent period or 3 months, whichever is less.

Evictions - Eviction Action

1) Eviction Action Complaint

2) Summons

3) Affidavit of Military Service

3) Writ of Possession

Mississippi

Non-Payment - 3 days.

Infractions of the Lease - 30 days.

End of Tenancy - 30 days.

Evictions - Unlawful Entry and Detainer

1) Complaint

2) Summons

3) Writ of Possession

Missouri

Non-Payment - Landlord may obtain summons upon failure to pay.

Infractions of the Lease - 7 days to remedy, 30 days if not cured.

End of Tenancy - 30 days or specified otherwise in lease.

Evictions - Unlawful Entry and Detainer

1) Complaint

2) Summons

3) Order for Possession (Writ of Restitution]

Montana

Non-Payment - 3 days.

Infractions of the Lease - 14 days

End of Tenancy - 30 days.

Evictions - Unlawful Entry and Detainer

1) Complaint

2) Summons

3) Writ of Possession

Nebraska

Non-Payment - 3 days.

Infractions of the Lease - 14 days.

End of Tenancy - 30 days.

Evictions - Unlawful Entry and Detainer

1) Complaint

2) Summons

3) Writ of Possession

Nevada

Non-Payment - 5 days.

Infractions of the Lease - 5 days—Tenant has only 3 days after service to comply—redeem tenancy.

End of Tenancy - 30 days.

Evictions - Unlawful Detainer Action

Summary Eviction (Possession Only)

1) Complaint

2) Summons

3) Writ of Restitution (Execution)

New Hampshire

Non-Payment - 7 days

Infractions of the Lease - 30 days

End of Tenancy - 30 days

Evictions - Unlawful Detainer

1) Writ (Sheriff)

2) Complaint

3) Summons

New Jersey

Non-Payment - No notice rule.

Infractions of the Lease - 30 days

End of Tenancy - 30 days

Evictions - Summary Proceedings

1) Complaint

2) Summons

3) Judgment for Possession

4) Warrant of Possession

New Mexico

Non-Payment - 3 days.

Infractions of the Lease - 7 days

End of Tenancy - 30 days.

Evictions - Petition for Writ of Restitution (PFWOR)

1) Complaint

2) Summons

3) Writ of Restitution

New York

Non-Payment - 3 days

Infractions of the Lease - 30 days

End of Tenancy - 30 days

Evictions - Summary Proceedings

1) Cover Sheet

2) Notice of Petition

3) Petition

North Carolina

Non-Payment - 10 days

Infractions of the Lease - 10 days

End of Tenancy - 30 days

Evictions - Summary Ejectment Action

1) Complaint for Summary Ejectment (possession only).

2) Complaint for Summary Ejectment

3) Writ of Possession

North Dakota

Non-Payment - 3 days

Infractions of the Lease - 10 days

End of Tenancy - 30 days

Evictions - Unlawful Detainer

1) Complaint

2) Summons

3) Writ of Possession

Ohio

Non-Payment - 3 days

Infractions of the Lease - 3 days

End of Tenancy - 30 days

Evictions - Unlawful and Forcible Entry

1) Complaint

2) Summons

3) Writ of Restitution

Oklahoma

Non-Payment - 5 days

Infractions of the Lease - 10 days

End of Tenancy - 30 days

Evictions - Forcible Entry and Detainer

1) Petition

2) Summons

3) Writ of Restitution

Oregon

Non-Payment - 3 days served after the rent is 8 days late

Infractions of the Lease - 10 days

End of Tenancy - 30 days less than a year, 60 days if over a year

Evictions - Forcible Entry and Detainer

1) Complaint

2) Summons

3) Affidavit of Military Service

4) Notice of Restitution

Pennsylvania

Non-Payment - 10 days

Infractions of the Lease - 15 days

End of Tenancy - Less than a year -5 days. More than a year - 30 days

 Evictions - Eviction Complaint

1) Complaint

2) Summons

3) Writ of Possession

Rhode Island

Non-Payment - 5 days served no sooner than 15 days after rent is in arrears.

Infractions of the Lease - A notice specifying the breach and demanding cure within 20 days from date

End of Tenancy - 30 days

Evictions - Unlawful Detainer

1) Complaint

2) Summons

3) Writ of Restitution

South Carolina

Non-Payment - 5 days

Infractions of the Lease - 14 days

End of Tenancy - 30 days

Evictions - Ejectment Action

1) Application for Ejectment

2) Affidavit

3) Writ of Ejectment

South Dakota

Non-Payment - 3 days

Infractions of the Lease - Reasonable notice to cure

End of Tenancy - At least as long before the conclusion of each rental period as the length of the period itself

Evictions - Forcible Entry Lawsuit

1) Complaint

2) Summons

3) Execution of Possession

Tennessee

Non-Payment - Under the Uniform Residential Landlord and Tenant act - 30 days, unless lease specifies no notice required. If not under URLT Act 14 days

Infractions of the Lease - 14 days to cure and termination of lease on 30th day after service if not cured

End of Tenancy - 30 days

Evictions - Forcible Entry and Detainer

1) Detainer Warrant

2) Writ of Possession

Texas

Non-Payment - Lease must specify "3 days".

Infractions of the Lease - 3 days. If lease provides for time to cure, such time must be provided before eviction notice may be given.

End of Tenancy - 30 days

Evictions - Forcible Entry and Detainer

1) Complaint

2) Summons

3) Writ of Restitution

Utah

Non-Payment - 3 days

Infractions of the Lease - 15 days

End of Tenancy - 15 days

Evictions - Forcible Entry and Detainer

1) Complaint

2) Summons

3) Appearance (tenant)

4) Writ of Restitution

Vermont

Non-Payment - 14 days

Infractions of the Lease - 30 days

End of Tenancy - 60 days for resident 2 years or less, 90 days over 2 years

Evictions - Forcible Entry and Detainer

1) Complaint

2) Summons

3) Writ of Restitution

Virginia

Non-Payment - 5 days

Infractions of the Lease - None, landlord can proceed in court for determination of right to re-entry.

End of Tenancy - 30 days

Evictions - Unlawful Detainer

1) Complaint

2) Summons

3) Affidavit of Military Service

4) Writ of Restitution

Washington

Non-Payment - 3 days

Infractions of the Lease - 10 days

End of Tenancy - 20 days

Evictions - Unlawful Detainer

1) Complaint

2) Summons

3) Writ of Restitution

West Virginia

Non-Payment - None, landlord may proceed with action in Ejectment or Eviction

Infractions of the Lease - Amount of time should be specified in the lease

End of Tenancy - Year to year - 90 days

Evictions - Summary Ejectment

1) Complaint

2) Summons

3) Writ of Restitution (Possession)

Wisconsin

Non-Payment - 5 days. If lease is over one year - 30 days.
Tenancy is terminated if a notice of termination is given at least
14 days after rent is due.

Infractions of the Lease - 5 days. If lease is over one year - 30 days

End of Tenancy - 28 days

1) Complaint

2) Summons

3) Writ of Restitution

Wyoming

Non-Payment - 3 days when an unconditional demand for
possession is made. Rent must be at least 3 days in arrears

Infractions of the Lease - 3 days unconditional demand for
possession

End of Tenancy - 28 days

1) Complaint

2) Summons

3) Writ of Possession

Quit or Pay, Breaking of Lease and End of Tenancy Notices

We feel the most powerful tool in obtaining your rent is serving the Quit or Pay Notices. Being a landlord is a business so we don't want to waste our time serving courtesy notices. The tenant knows it is due and we want the money! If you want to make friends be sure to join a bike club not being a landlord

What it does for us is puts the pressure on the tenants, which in turn takes the pressure off of our shoulders. When we serve our Quit or Pay Notices including late fee, it sends out the message; —WE WANT OUR RENT or you'll have to move‖. We serve our Quit or Pay Notice on the 7th so our tenants know exactly the amount due and the time frame in which they have to pay.

We serve the Breaking of Lease Notice when a tenant has broken our lease. Just a suggestion but we always read the rules and regulations to the new tenant at lease signing. This way we know they are aware we don't put up disruption

End of Tenancy Notice is to be served before due date to end the month to month tenancy

Quit or Pay Notice:

On the 7th of the month we serve our **quit or pay notices**. Most tenants live week to week or otherwise they would have bought a home not rented. We will bend but not break

We make a copy of the notice before serving. We serve the tenant or any person over 13 yrs. of age that lives at the residence. Then we go to a notary public and have our copy notarized and fill in the date and person receiving the notice. If the tenant pays the amount within the time allotted, we can't proceed to the Eviction. We must accept the rent.

Breaking of Lease Notice:

We use this notice if a tenant has broken one of the stipulations in our lease. Just as the 5-Day Notice, if they comply with complaint, we can't go forward for an Eviction.

If they don't comply, we take the **breaking of lease notice** to Circuit Clerk's office to obtain an Eviction court date. We will be asking for court costs and possession, but no money judgment (a separate lawsuit has to be filed in Small Claims Court to obtain a money judgment),

End of Tenancy Notice:

Serve the **end of tenancy notice** before due date to end the tenancy at the end of the upcoming month. We serve it on a month to month lease or on a tenant after the year lease has expired and are now holding over.

Quit of Pay

Notice Non-Payment of Rent

(Example on Next Page)

In most states there is no grace period pertaining to the serving of the **quit or pay notice**.

In a few states, you cannot serve **a quit or pay notice** until a certain amount of days after rent is due.

This document is a *quit or pay notice*, which can be served by the plaintiff to the defendant not needing a process server.

This states how much rent is due as of that date stated on notice. A copy is made before giving the notice to the tenant. Our copy must be notarized the day it is served.

We like to do our talking with our notices. The quicker you serve your **quit or pay notices** the better. Don't waste time with courtesy calls or letters.

The **quit or pay notice** is notarized and is time sensitive. This says —We mean business.

We like to show the tenant the **quit or pay notice** when they move in and sign the lease. Explain to them how it will be used in the non-payment of rent.

Explain that it just means I need the rent. It doesn't say we are the bad guy and we want the tenant to move. It simply states we want the rent.

Quit or Pay Notice

Date of service ***Date the notice was served***,

TO: ***Name of Person(s) on the rental agreement***_____

FROM: ***Name of landlord or rental manager***_____

Your rent being in arrears, you are hereby notified to quit and deliver **amount of days** from receipt of this notice to pay in full the amount owed in rent **amount owed in rent** by **date amount has to paid.**

The premises now held by you as my tenant namely:

Complete address_____

Print Name of Landlord or Rental Agent

Signature of Landlord or Rental Agent

Complete address of Landlord or Rental Agent

Notary Public_____

10 - Day Notice Infractions of the Lease

(Example on Next Page)

This document is served to the tenant when a violation of the lease is broken—this notice is served to the tenant by the landlord. A copy is made before serving the notice. Our copy is notarized the day we serve the notice.

The tenant has **state specific statute** to correct the infractions. If after time allotted the infractions aren't corrected, we will obtain an Eviction court hearing for court costs and possession (only).

 Any money owed will have to be sought in a separate lawsuit in Small Claims Court.

Remember that the breaking of lease notice concerns violations or infractions of the lease only, and does not deal with rent due at all. Any violations or infractions listed on a breaking of lease notice must be against a specific rule or regulation set forth in the written agreement.

Breaking of Lease Notice

(Cure)

To: Name of Person(s) on Lease **Names of Person(s) on lease**

You are hereby notified that (cite non-compliance):

State infraction of lease *State the infraction of the lease*

Demand is hereby made that you remedy the non-compliance within **state specific statute** of receipt of this notice or your tenancy or lease shall be deemed terminated and you shall vacate upon termination.

If this conduct of a similar nature is repeated within 12 months, your tenancy is subject to termination without being given an opportunity to cure.

Date of filing **date of filing**

Print name of Landlord **print name of landlord**

Signature of Landlord **signature of landlord**

Complete address **complete address of landlord**

Contact number **contact number of landlord**

Notary Public **notarized**

BREAKING OF LEASE NOTICE

(No cure)

TO: **Tenant name and all unknown occupants**

Complete address of rental property_____

You are hereby notified that, in consequence of your default under the provisions of the lease, specifically **infractions against the rules and regulations in the rental agreement**_____

_____

You are notified that the infraction was the second time in 12 months. Your lease will be terminated and you will deliver the possession of the property immediately.

Date of service

Signature of landlord_

End of Tenancy Notice

(Example on Next Page)

The **end of tenancy notice** has to be served by the plaintiff prior to due date of the rent to end a month-to-month tenancy or to end a year lease.

For instance, if the rent is due April 1, then we would have to serve this document March 31 to end the tenancy April 30.

This document can be served by the landlord. A copy is made before serving the notice to the tenant. Our copy is notarized the date we serve it.

The **end of tenancy notice** can be a very helpful tool when dealing with problematic tenants.

We can decide to enter into a month-to-month tenancy where either party can end the tenancy with the serving of a 30-Day Notice. We give up the security of the year lease, but can now end the tenancy for basically no reason other than you want possession. So, if things get out of hand and the tenants are dealing drugs, or damaging your property or moving other people in or disturbing the neighbors, all you have to do is serve an **end of tenancy notice** without pointing fingers.

If they then do not pay the rent, knowing they will be moving, we can serve a **quit or pay notice** for non-payment. This takes precedence over the **end of tenancy notice**

END OF TENANCY NOTICE

TO: **Tenant name an all unknown occupants**

-   **Complete address of rental property___**

You are hereby notified that your lease for the property located at: **Complete address of rental property**

_____

Will be terminated as **6/1/2020**   you must turn over the possession of the property to me at that time

.

No further demand shall be necessary before bringing legal proceedings to recover the premises.

Date of service

Signature of landlord

Affidavit of Military Service

With any default judgment granted in the Eviction or Small Claims Court, the judge will request an Affidavit of Military Service. Also, when a Bench Warrant is issued in the Citation Court, an Affidavit of Military Service is needed.

Before the court proceeding in any of the three courts (Eviction, Small Claims, or Discovery) we pick up an Affidavit of Military Service form at the Circuits Clerk's office.

On your local courthouse website, there is a self-help center that allows us to go on-line to the Department of Defense's web-site to produce data that show whether the defendant(s) are in the military.

The Department of Defense requires a birth date and middle initial or social security number. The Department of Defense will print out a document stating their findings.

Fill out the Affidavit of Military Service. Be sure to sign and date it. Attach it to the Department of Defense data sheet, and present both documents to the judge when needed.

Eviction

The 6 examples below present common scenarios that occur in the Forcible Detainer or Eviction Court.

1) **Defendant(s) served**

   Defendant(s) appear

When our case is called, we proceed to the podium. The judge will ask you to identify yourself, defendant and plaintiff. To represent yourself, your name has to be one of the plaintiff's.

The judge will ask, —Do you have proof of service? (Not the invoice receipt). We hand the judge our proof of services that we had picked up at the process server prior to court.

The judge will examine the **quit or pay notice** (already in the court files) and the proof of service.

Judge will ask you "what are you asking for in your Eviction?"

Reply, —The amount of rent, plus 7 more days, court costs, possession in 7 days.

Defendant will have a chance to agree or disagree. If they agree, fill in the three appropriate spaces on form, rent, court costs, and possession. Hand the judge order to sign. He/she will sign and rip off the top white sheet to stay in the court files, handing the canary copy to defendant, and the pink copy to the plaintiff). Proceed to the Circuit Clerk's office with the order to schedule the sheriff for removal and to obtain one of the three avenues of post - judgment proceedings.

2) Defendant(s) served

Defendant(s) appear

Admit to owing, but wants to pay judgment and stay in residence

We have accepted the money from the defendant after the judgment had been decided in the *Eviction*. The tenant has to pay in full the rent and late fees plus court costs.

3) Defendant enter a *motion* to vacate money judgment.

We will receive a notice through the mail stating that the defendant(s) have filed a *motion* to vacate money judgment. This automatically stops the sheriff from removing the defendant. At the *motion*, the judge will review any new evidence to reverse his/her decision.

If the plaintiffs followed all the procedures, the judge will deny the *motion*. Have the extra rent amount calculated from the time of this first possession date, to the date of the *motion*. Ask the judge to grant the extra amount of rent due.

4) Defendant(s) served

Defendant(s) fail to appear

Not in military

Follow the procedure - **Eviction** (1) but when the judge asks for proof of service of **Complaint and Summons**, you will hand the judge the **Affidavit of Military Service** with the proof of service, showing that the defendant(s) are not in the military service

5) **Defendant(s) served**

Defendant(s) appear

Admit to owing, but ask for more time

The judge will usually ask us if we have any objections to giving the defendant more time to vacate. That's the time we explain that the defendant(s) have been living in the residence since (the first day of non-payment). We ask the courts to grant our plea of seven days to vacate (amount of —stay awarded).

 If the judge gives the defendant more time, be sure to have the daily amount of rent to add to the original amount of rent owed.

6) **Defendant(s) non-service**

Proceed to follow **Eviction** (1) but when asked by the judge if the defendant was served, reply —No, judge then hand the non-service to the judge. He/she will ask, —What are you seeking **Alias** or **Post**?

Eviction Process Non-Service "Alias"

Alias - Means continuing the lawsuit asking for a money judgment and possession.

When we know of the defendant(s) whereabouts we will obtain the Alias Forcible Detainer at the Circuit Clerk's office. We will have to serve the defendant(s) the Alias Forcible Detainer

(Alias Summons). The rent accrued from the first return to court, to the date of possession in

Alias Forcible Detainer, will be added on the original amount.

Post - Means we surrender the money judgment for just possession. The judge will instruct you to proceed to the Circuit Clerk's office for appropriate Posting forms. The Circuit Clerk fills it in. The sheriff posts the documents on the residence and public areas that state the court time and place of posting hearing. The court date that the judge grants at the podium is usually two weeks. At the Posting hearing the judge will render possession that day.

Then to seek a money judgment we have to file a separate lawsuit in Small Claims Court.

Eviction Process

1) Cover Sheet

Stays in court files. States what type of case—plaintiff and defendant plus how much money is being sought and if the plaintiff is suing for court costs.

2) Complaint

This document is one of the two documents that have to be served to the defendant by a licensed process server or the sheriff. The other document is the **Summons**. Both state money being sought, court date, time and court costs.

3) Summons

As the **Complaint**, this document has to be served. The judge will ask for —proof of service of this document along with **complaint**.

4) Order

When judge awards rent, court costs, and possession, we will fill in appropriate spaces.

This is the document we take to the Circuit Clerk to schedule the sheriff for removal and proceed with to —Post-Judgment proceedings.

Case type **Eviction**

Case no **Clerk will award**

Maximum Claim amount **rent, court costs & accrued rent**

COVER SHEET

Person or party suing   **Person or party being sued**

Complete address   **complete address**

_____   _____

Attorney for the Plaintiff or Pro Se **name of attorney or landlord**

Address of attorney or landlord _____

Filed this _____

First Return Date _____

Print name of Person or Party suing   Case No. **Clerk awarded**

Print mane of Person or Party being sued

Name of Person or Party suing_____ complain that the said plaintiff is entitled to the possession of the following premise **complete address of rental property**_____

COMPLAINT

And that the **name of Person or Party being sued**_____

Unlawfully withhold possession thereof from the said Plaintiff for rent of said premises in the sum of **rent due, court costs, accrued rent**.

Wherefore, Plaintiff prays that a Summons issued in pursuance of the Statute, returnable on ___**clerk will award**___

Date of filing_____

Person or Party suing

Signature of attorney or landlord

To each Defendant: **Name of Person being sued**

SUMMONS

YOU ARE HEREBY SUMMONED and required to appear before this court at **Name and address of courthouse** at _____ o'clock, on **clerk will award** to answer the complaint in this case, a copy of which is attached. IF YOU FAIL TO DO SO, A JUDGMENT BY DEFAULT MAY BE TAKEN AGAINST YOU FOR THE RELIEF ASKED IN THE COMPLAINT.

NOTICE TO DEFENDANT

This case will not go to trial on the day specified above: On the day for appearance specified above, the following will occur:

A. You have not obeyed the Summons, a judgment may be entered against for the relief stated on the Complaint.

B. If you entered an appearance or filed an Answer, your case will be set over for a trial, at that time you must be present and prepared for trial.

C. If you appear you will be asked to admit or deny the allegations.

D. If you appear and FAILED TO PAY THE REQUIRED FILING FEE, UNLESS A PREVIOUSLY GRANTED FILING FEE WAIVER FOR THIS CASE IS IN THE FILE, A JUDGMENT DEFAULT MAY BE TAKEN AGAINST YOU FOR THE RELIEF ASKED FOR IN THE COMPLAINT.

Person or Party suing _____

Person or Party being sued ____   Case No. **Clerk will award**

ORDER

1.Judgment is entered in favor of Plaintiff/Defendant **Person or Party suing** against **Person or Party being sued**/ Plaintiff in the amount of **awarded by Judge** plus court costs in the amount of **awarded by Judge** together with attorney's fees in the amount of **attorney's fees.**

2. The court further orders that possession of the premises located at **address of rental property** _____shall be restored to the Plaintiff by **date they have to move awarded by the Judge.**

TO THE SHERIFF OF **name of County**

You are commanded pursuant to the judgment of this court to restore **Person or Party suing** ____ to the possession and to remove **Person or Party being sued and all unknown occupants** from the possession of the premises **address of rental property**

Date **Judge**

Entered **Judge**

1) **Alias Summons**

This form is what you will fill out and have served by the process server or sheriff, if we want another opportunity to have the defendant appear for the **Eviction Court**.

2) **Posting Notice**

This form along with the form below is filled out at the Circuit Clerks office. You are giving up a money judgment to regain possession. To be awarded a money judgment you will file a Small Claims court case.

They are given to the sheriff to post on the door of the property, and in the court house.

3) **Posting Affidavit**

This form accompanies the form above in the **Posting** process the **Eviction Court.**

TRIAL

The defendant has the right to plead their case in a trial if they disagree with the plaintiff's allegations at the First Return, meaning the first time you were in court with this case.

Be prepared to support your case bring these documents to your trial. Do not bring pictures of damages because you are suing for rent. Don't get the judge upset by not being aware of your statutes.

There is a few states that allow damages in Eviction so check your state statute

Lease

Rental receipts.

Order you received when you filed for the **Eviction**.

Eviction notice

Proof of service will already be in the court files.

1) **Defendant appears**

   Paid filing fee to participate

Judge will ask both parties to identify themselves. He/she will open the trial with the plaintiff explaining the amount of rent due up to today, the amount of court costs accrued (cost of **Eviction** and cost of service), and date that we are asking for to obtain possession.

He/she will ask for a copy of the **lease** to verify the address, rent amount, month to month or year lease, etc.

The defendant will have their time to plead their position. Judge will make a decision.

You must fill in the appropriate spaces on the **order** and hand it to the judge to sign.

2) **Defendant appears**

   Did not pay filing fee to participate

The judge will award a default judgment. Fill in appropriate spaces on the **order** when the judge grants the rent, court costs, and possession. Hand to the judge to sign.

He/she will rip off top white sheet, handing us the canary/pink sheet.

3) **Defendant fails to appear**

The judge will award a default judgment which means we will need an Affidavit of Military Service on both defendants.

www.ingramcontent.com/pod-product-compliance
Lightning Source LLC
Chambersburg PA
CBHW030525220526
45463CB00007B/2723